Seeds by Wind and Water

Helene J. Jordan
Illustrated by Nils Hogner

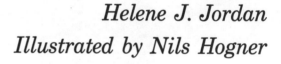

THOMAS Y. CROWELL COMPANY
NEW YORK

Birds fly, animals run, fish swim
    to get from one place to another.
We know that.

Seeds move from one place to another, too.
Let's find out how.

Sometimes we move seeds ourselves.

We buy seeds and put them in the ground.
We buy sunflower seeds and carrot seeds.
We buy morning glory seeds and radish seeds.
We put them in the garden
   where we want the plants to grow.

Plants grow in the woods, too.
Plants grow in the fields,
   on the mountains,
   in wet places,
   and in dry places.

But no one puts those seeds
   in the ground.

Plants grow from seeds that go from place to place
through the air, over the ground,
on top of the water.

Let's find out how they travel.

This is a dandelion when it is yellow.

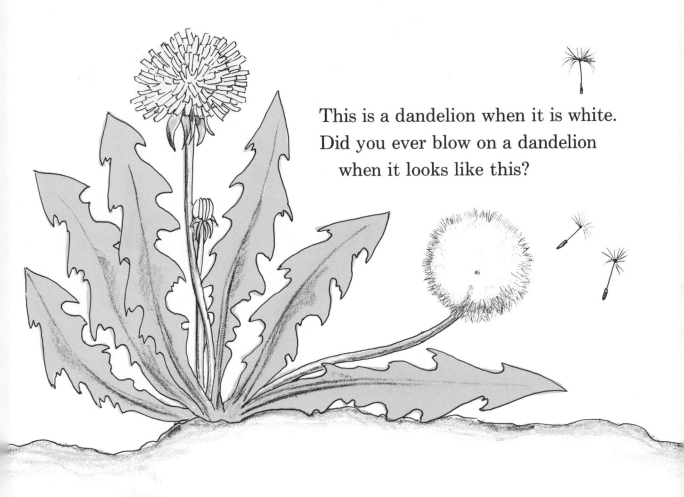

This is a dandelion when it is white.
Did you ever blow on a dandelion
when it looks like this?

Try it some time.
 It comes apart into little pieces of fluff.
 Each bit of fluff looks like a white umbrella.
 At the bottom of each umbrella is a seed.
The wind blows the fluff away.
The wind blows the seed away.

When the wind stops blowing,
 the umbrella and the seed
 come down to the ground.
If the seed settles into the earth
 some day another dandelion may grow.

This is the seed of a maple tree.
It has wings on it.
The wings carry the seed along on the wind.
It may go far from the maple tree.

When the wind stops blowing,
the seed falls to the ground.

Some day a maple tree may grow from it.

Seeds of milkweed, of thistle,
  of ash and elm trees
  are carried through the air by the wind.

Seeds are carried by birds, too.

Birds eat blueberries or cherries,
raspberries or blackberries.

Later, they drop the seeds,
and new plants grow from them.

Birds carry seeds in other ways.
Seeds may fall into the mud
   at the edges of streams and lakes.
Sandpipers wade in the mud.
   The mud and seeds stick to their feet.

The birds carry the seeds
   to the edge of another stream.
Some of them wash off
   and grow into new plants along the shore.

Even your dog can help move seeds. So can your cat.
A dog chases a rabbit through a field.
    A cat hunts a mouse in the yard.
Seeds from grass and other plants stick to their fur.

Sometimes the seeds are in burs
with little hooks on them, like this.

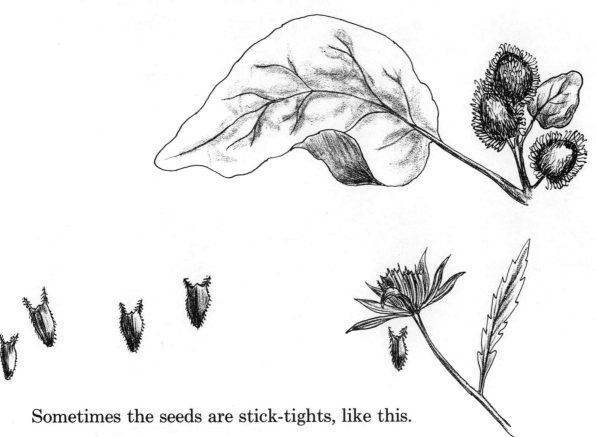

Sometimes the seeds are stick-tights, like this.

When the seeds fall from the burs or stick-tights,
    a new plant may grow.
Have you ever had burs or stick-tights on your clothes?
Did you pull them off and throw them away?
Then YOU helped seeds to travel.

Squirrels carry seeds, too.
They fill holes with acorns, hickory nuts,
   and other seeds to eat during the winter.

Sometimes the squirrels forget where they hid the seeds.
Down in the hole the seeds begin to grow.
An oak tree or a hickory tree
may grow from seeds that a squirrel forgot.

Some plants move their own seeds.
  The seeds are in a pod.
When the pod dries out it splits open.
  The seeds pop out.
Violet seeds pop.

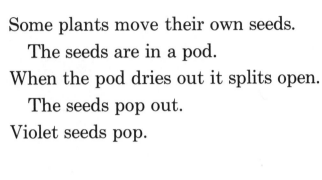

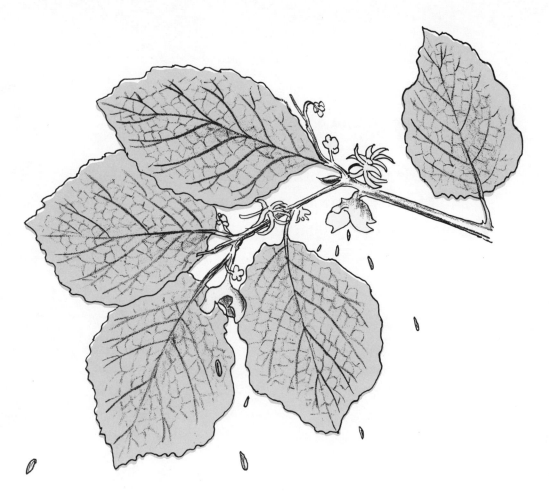

Touch-me-not seeds pop.
And so do witch-hazel seeds.

Seeds are moved in other ways.

Some seeds fall into brooks and rivers
and are carried away. A willow tree may grow
from a seed that floated down a stream.

Some seeds fall into the ocean and are carried away.
A palm tree may grow from a coconut
that floated for many miles.

Seeds catch in the tires of an automobile.
They drop out in the next town,
or even in the next state.

Then new plants grow.

Seeds are carried by airplane tires far across oceans.
When they drop out of the tires
they grow into plants in another country.

Now you know many ways that seeds travel.

They are carried

by the wind,

by streams,

by dogs and cats,

by birds,

and even by you.

Some plants move their own seeds.

Even automobiles and airplanes
carry seeds.

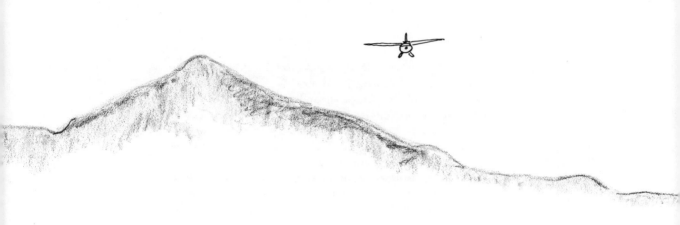

That is why you see plants
   in low fields and on high mountains,
   in wet places and in dry places.
They grow from seeds no one planted.
But they grow so well that trees and flowers
   are all around you.

ABOUT THE AUTHOR

HELENE J. JORDAN was born and educated in Grand Rapids, Michigan. She has taught speech and drama to young people and has written and directed for radio. She has written extensively for various magazines and newspapers and is now an associate editor of *Natural History*, the magazine of the American Museum of Natural History.

Mrs. Jordan enjoys fishing, listening to her hi-fi, reading, and watching the deer in her garden. Her interest in photographing plants in their various stages of growth led to the writing of her first book, *How a Seed Grows*, and *Seeds by Wind and Water*.

ABOUT THE ILLUSTRATOR

NILS HOGNER and his wife, Dorothy Hogner, have an herb farm in Litchfield, Connecticut, where they "raise everything from basil to sweet cicely in the field and in planter boxes!"

Nils Hogner is an active member of the National Society of Mural Painters and the Architectural League of New York. Mr. Hogner is primarily a mural painter. His Memorial to the Four Chaplains may be seen at Temple University in Philadelphia. He also works in the art technique of architectural porcelain on steel, as well as the art of illustration for his own and his wife's books.